INSTITUTE OF LEADERSHIP & MANAGEMENT **ilm**

SUPERSERIES

Appraising Performance

FOURTH EDITION

Published for the
Institute of Leadership & Management by

Pergamon
Flexible
Learning

OXFORD AMSTERDAM BOSTON LONDON NEW YORK PARIS
SAN DIEGO SAN FRANCISCO SINGAPORE SYDNEY TOKYO

Pergamon Flexible Learning
An imprint of Elsevier
Linacre House, Jordan Hill, Oxford OX2 8DP
200 Wheeler Road, Burlington, MA 01803

First published 1986
Second edition 1991
Third edition 1997
Fourth edition 2003
Reprinted 2003, 2004

Copyright © 1986, 1991, 1997, 2003, ILM
All rights reserved.

No part of this publication may be reproduced in any material form (including photocopying or storing in any medium byelectronic means and whether or not transiently or incidentally to some other use of this publication) without the written permission of the copyright holder except in accordance with the provisions of the Copyright,Designs and Patents Act 1988 or under the terms of a licence issued by the Copyright Licensing Agency Ltd, 90 Tottenham Court Road, London, England W1T 4LP. Applications for the copyright holder's written permission to reproduce any part of this publication should be addressed to the publisher.

Permissions may be sought directly from Elsevier's Science and Technology Rights Department in Oxford, UK: phone: (+44) 1865 843830; fax: (+44) 1865 853333; e-mail: permissions@elsevier.co.uk. You may also complete your request on-line via the Elsevier homepage (http://www.elsevier.com), by selecting 'Customer Support' and then 'Obtaining Permissions'.

British Library Cataloguing in Publication Data
A catalogue record for this book is available from the British Library

ISBN 0 7506 5838 X

For information on Pergamon Flexible Learning
visit our website at www.bh.com/pergamonfl

Institute of Leadership & Management
registered office
1 Giltspur Street
London
EC1A 9DD
Telephone 020 7294 3053
www.i-l-m.com
ILM is a subsidiary of the City & Guilds Group

The views expressed in this work are those of the authors and do not necessarily reflect those of the Institute of Leadership & Management or of the publisher

Authors: Alison Allenby and Dela Jenkins
Editor: Dela Jenkins
Editorial management: Genesys, www.genesys-consultants.com
Based on previous material by: Alison Allenby
Composition by Genesis Typesetting, Rochester, Kent
Printed and bound in Great Britain by MPG Books Ltd, Bodmin, Cornwall

Contents

Contents

Workbook introduction

1 ILM Super Series study links

This workbook addresses the issues of *Appraising Performance*. Should you wish to extend your study to other Super Series workbooks covering related or different subject areas, you will find a comprehensive list at the back of this book.

2 Links to ILM Qualifications

This workbook relates to the following learning outcomes in segments from the ILM Level 3 Introductory Certificate in First Line Management and the Level 3 Certificate in First Line Management.

C7.8 Assessing Performance
1 Appreciate the value of assessing performance to the organization and individuals
2 Ensure individuals have fair access, and an opportunity to contribute, to assessment
3 Plan and prepare effective assessments against agreed criteria
4 Make valid and reliable assessments
5 Provide feedback to individuals on their performance and development
6 Provide information on assessments to authorized people only
7 Maintain appropriate assessment records

C8.2 Managing Performance
3 Review performance and agree improvements
4 Monitor performance against objectives

C9.4 Giving and receiving feedback
3 Use feedback to improve the performance of others

3 Links to S/NVQs in Management

This workbook relates to the following elements of the Management Standards which are used in S/NVQs in Management, as well as a range of other S/NVQs.

C12.2 Assess the work of teams and individuals
C12.3 Provide feedback to teams and individuals on their work.

It will also help you to develop the following Personal Competences:

- building teams
- communicating
- thinking and taking decisions.

4 Workbook objectives

All organizations need information on how their employees are performing and developing so that the future human resource planning and budgeting needs of the organization can be met. It is also important to individuals that they are given some feedback about the work they carry out. They need to know what they do well. This motivates them and helps them to realize that their value is appreciated. They also need to know where their performance needs to be improved. If they don't know this then they cannot improve.

Appraisal systems provide the information that both organizations and individuals need to know about performance. However, the type of system and the techniques used vary considerably from one organization to the next. Indeed some organizations may have no formal performance appraisal system at all.

In this workbook we will help you to understand the meaning of performance appraisal and the different uses that are made of it. The workbook will also assist you to contribute effectively to the performance appraisal system used in your own organization.

It will also assist you in assessing the effectiveness of your existing systems and perhaps making some recommendations for ways in which both systems and documentation could be improved.

4.1 Objectives

When you have worked through this workbook you will be better able to:

- define performance appraisal, its aims, purposes and benefits;
- plan and prepare for a performance appraisal interview;
- agree performance objectives;
- make valid and reliable assessments;
- assess the job skills and personal qualities of staff;
- identify training and development needs;
- ask appropriate interview questions;
- listen to employees during interviews;
- give effective feedback on performance;
- draw up action plans;
- monitor performance against objectives;
- select appropriate methods to improve performance where necessary;
- complete appraisal documentation.

5 Activity planner

The following Activities need some planning and you may want to look at them now.

Activity 17 asks you to complete a Personal Qualities Appraisal Form for one of your workteam.

Activity 18 requires you to record some details about an informal or formal observation on your workteam carrying out a task.

Activity 19 asks you to give some information about two occasions when you have had to examine the work of your workteam.

Activity 25 questions you about any occasion when you have given a member of your workteam the opportunity to assess his or her own work.

Activity 33 requires you to complete an action plan showing a development area for a member of your workteam.

Activity 35 requires you to discuss with a member of your workteam and agree performance ratings on the three objectives set in Activity 17.

Activity 37 suggests that you rate the telephone behaviour of a member of your workteam.

Activity 38 advises you to complete a narrative appraisal report for one of your workteam.

Some or all of these Activities may provide the basis of evidence for your S/NVQ portfolio. All Portfolio Activities and the Work-based assignment are signposted with this icon.

The icon states the elements to which the Portfolio Activities and Work-based assignment relate.

Session A
The aims and objectives of appraisal

1 Introduction

All organizations need to know how well their personnel are performing. They need a system that regularly measures achievement against set targets and identifies and remedies any shortfalls against these targets.

The number of organizations running formal appraisal systems has steadily increased over the last ten years. In fact it has been estimated that over 80 per cent of organizations have some system for formally appraising their staff. There has also been a significant increase in the number of non-managerial employees being appraised. Along with this increase in the number of people receiving appraisals there has obviously also been an increase in the number of first line managers being required to run appraisals. Never has it been more important to develop the necessary skills to ensure that appraisals are run effectively.

In this first session we will look at what is meant by appraisal, and its significance, both to the organization and to an individual. We will also look at the purpose of appraisals and examine the issues that are raised and discussed in an appraisal interview.

The personnel responsible for conducting appraisal interviews will vary from one organization to another. However, in the majority of organizations the first line manager responsible for the performance of a particular workteam is the person who carries out the appraisal interview for that team. In addition to any formal system that the first line manager may be responsible for, it is also essential that informal appraisal is carried out all the time.

2 Defining performance appraisal

Performance appraisal can be defined as any procedure which helps the collecting, sharing, giving and using of information collected from, and about, people at work in order to add to their performance.

So we can say that appraisal is a tool that is used to improve an organization's performance by making better use of its people and by improving their individual performances.

Activity 1 · 3 mins

Jot down at least **three** ways in which you could collect, check, share, give or use information from your workteam for the purpose of adding to their performance at work.

_____

_____

_____

You may have thought of many different examples, such as:

■ keeping up-to-date records;
■ monitoring progress of training programmes;
■ running briefing sessions;
■ giving instructions and making sure they are carried out;
■ giving feedback on how a particular job has been done;
■ checking time cards or overtime claims;
■ monitoring attendance.

You can see from this that appraisal is a very varied activity and is something we are involved in all the time.

In addition to the informal methods we have just described many organizations also organize formal performance appraisals. These often take place within the context of an annual performance appraisal interview.

3 The benefits of performance appraisal

Performance appraisal provides many benefits to both the organization and the employees concerned.

Activity 2 · 4 mins

List **four** benefits that you think performance appraisal could produce for a first line manager.

_____

_____

_____

_____

There are many benefits to you as a first line manager. Here are some of them.

- It provides an opportunity for you to discuss an employee's performance at work.
- It enables you to give positive feedback to an employee on work completed to a high standard.
- It provides an opportunity for you to identify any training needs the employee may have.
- It produces a record of the employee's performance at work.
- It enables you to negotiate and agree work targets and objectives for the employee to work towards during the next period.

- It identifies any weaknesses the employee may have and looks for ways in which performance at work can be improved.
- It helps to clarify roles.

Many of these benefits are also benefits to the employees who are being appraised. There are, however, a few additional benefits for them to enjoy.

- Appraisal provides employees with an opportunity to discuss their job with their manager. They are able to say how they feel about things and to talk about the future.
- Many employees appreciate their manager showing an interest in their work and find it motivates them.
- Receiving positive feedback on work well done helps employees to realize that the work they do is appreciated and encourages them to work even harder in the future.

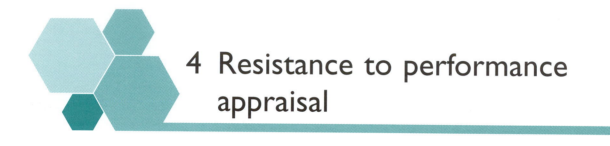

4 Resistance to performance appraisal

It may appear that feedback on performance assessment is inevitably going to be critical, and that it will only be used to point out things that are not being done properly.

However, this is not true. It is usually easy to think of some way in which performance can be improved but this isn't necessarily a criticism of performance to date. The dictionary defines an appraiser as one who values, and it is important to keep that in mind.

The aim of an appraisal is not to find fault, but to weigh up and evaluate performance, and the value we put on it should be very high. The whole direction of people's future careers may be strongly influenced by their appraisal at work.

Activity 3

5 mins

Jot down **three** reasons why you think people don't like having their performance appraised, and why they may resist the introduction of performance appraisal.

_____

_____

_____

_____

_____

_____

_____

_____

You have probably listed some reasons given by people in your present workplace or a previous workplace. These may include the fact that:

■ they don't believe that their manager is qualified to make judgements about them;
■ they fear that the information discussed will not be treated confidentially;
■ they feel that their first line manager is prejudiced or biased about them;
■ they think that their future within the organization may be curtailed;
■ they suspect that part of the appraisal is secret;
■ they consider that some aspects of performance are difficult to measure;
■ they believe that the admission of any failings will have a direct bearing on salary, especially when an organization operates a system of performance-related pay (PRP).

So we have established that appraisal schemes can meet with opposition from people who don't like having performance at work assessed. The reasons we have given so far are likely to be given by the people being appraised. But what about the managers and supervisors who carry out the appraisal? Many of them may have misgivings about an appraisal system too.

Activity 4 · 5 mins

Now try to think of **three** reasons why managers may not like appraising their employees' performance, and may resist the introduction of performance appraisal.

_____

_____

_____

_____

_____

_____

_____

You may have found the responses to the above activity more difficult than your responses to some of the previous activities, but here are some suggestions.

- managers may not feel comfortable when they are put in the position of 'playing god';
- appraisal may be time consuming and managers may believe they can make better use of their time;
- appraisal may produce a lot of paper;
- managers can become cynical of appraisal if there is no follow-up;
- managers may feel that appraisal interviews can result in poorer relationships with staff afterwards;
- managers may feel that it is very difficult to set and measure performance against objective standards;
- trade unions may be hostile to appraisal.

In spite of the possible resistance to performance appraisal, both by first line managers carrying out appraisals and by those whose performance is appraised, many organizations do operate appraisal systems. Many employers believe that the advantages are so great that they manage to minimize the disadvantages and successfully operate a system of performance appraisal.

There are a number of things that can happen to minimize the disadvantages of performance appraisal and ensure that the system operates successfully. Some of our ideas follow.

Organizations can make sure that:

- their first line managers are well trained to run appraisals;
- there is a right of appeal against any appraisal comment or marking that the employee does not agree with;
- paperwork systems are kept to a minimum.

First line managers can make sure that they:

- ensure appraisal is an ongoing process and not something that only happens formally once a year;
- plan and prepare for interviews;
- overcome any prejudice or bias they may have;
- build up trust with the people who work for them;
- use objective standards;
- give only constructive criticism.

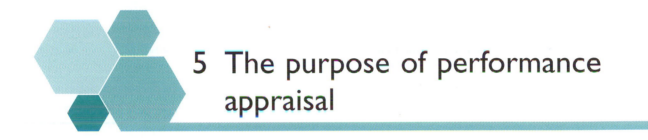

5 The purpose of performance appraisal

Performance appraisal has a variety of purposes which we will explore next.

Activity 5 · 4 mins

Write down **two** reasons why your organization might want to appraise the performance of its employees.

_____

_____

_____

_____

The two reasons you have given are probably included among these examples of purposes and objectives of appraisal:

- to supply management with data about staff capabilities, to help them with forecasting staff requirements and identifying potential;
- to evaluate staff training and personal development needs;
- to review past performance and determine the future of employees within the organization, for example, to decide which staff should be promoted;
- to motivate the employee by giving information about progress, recognizing achievement and encouraging feedback from staff;
- to set goals and prepare action plans to assist the career plans of employees;
- to determine wage and salary levels;
- to update employees' personnel records.

There are four parties who might wish to use the information generated by appraisal. They are as follows:

- the organization, and in particular, the human resources department or other functions within the organization;
- the appraiser (supervisor or first line manager);
- the supervisor or first line manager's manager;
- the person being appraised.

We can see that the information which results from performance appraisal is going to be used by various departments in the workplace. But how will it be used?

The table below was taken from *Performance Appraisal Revisited*, by P. Long, published by the Institute of Personnel Management. It gives the results of an investigation into the objectives that appraisers believe to be the main purposes of appraisal. The investigation involved 800 organizations.

Objective	Response (%)
To set performance objectives	81
To review past performance	98
To improve current performance	97
To assess training/development needs	97
To assess increases or new levels in salary	40
To assess future potential and promotability	71
To assist career planning decisions	75
Other	4

Overall, according to the study, the most important purposes of performance appraisal appear to be:

■ to review past performance;
■ to improve current performance;
■ to assess training and development needs;
■ to set performance objectives.

Let's go back to another 'interested party' for a moment and look at what the person being appraised hopes to achieve from the appraisal.

The goals of the individuals being appraised will, of course, vary, but possible goals are:

■ to impress the manager;
■ to increase the chances of a bonus payment or promotion;
■ to find out what the chances of promotion are;
■ to find out how their performance has been rated;
■ to find out what their weaknesses are;
■ to find out where they need to improve performance;
■ to get help in improving performance.

Sometimes there may be a problem when the objectives of the interested parties conflict. For example, the person being appraised and the human resources department may be looking for very different outcomes. However, ideally, appraisal should be part of a continuing dialogue between all the parties concerned, not the only opportunity they have to discuss widely varying interests and objectives, and as such should not be the focus for a head-on clash. Let us suppose the worst for a moment, though, and think about the sort of conflict of interests that could be highlighted by an appraisal.

Activity 6

4 mins

Write down an example of a situation where there may be a complete clash between the objectives of the person being appraised and the organization.

_____

_____

_____

_____

There are many possibilities and it's quite likely that we have thought of totally different examples, but here is one suggestion.

■ The organization may have the control of costs as one of its major objectives and will be using the appraisal system to help in this, perhaps by looking for ways of making more use of people's currently underused skills. The person being appraised may not be thinking in terms of a changed job but is hoping to secure a substantial pay rise as a result of the appraisal.

6 Aims and objectives of performance appraisal

Before starting performance appraisal it is important to be very clear about the aims of the exercise. Basically there are two areas to be appraised: the ability to perform to the requirements of the job, and behaviour in terms of attitude, attendance, timekeeping etc. We have already highlighted some of the main aims when assessing job performance. These are:

■ setting performance objectives;
■ assessing past performance and improving future performance;
■ assessing training and development needs;
■ assessing future potential;
■ determining salary.
■ developing individuals;
■ improving motivation;
■ providing job satisfaction.

We will now look at some of these in detail.

6.1 Setting performance objectives

Activity 7 · 4 mins

Take a few minutes to consider the performance objectives that you are expected to achieve. For example, at my place of work my manager expects me to turn around all student assignments within seven days.

Write down **two** examples of performance objectives that you expect your workteam to meet in its job.

_____

_____

_____

_____

_____

We are not able to give you specific feedback on your objectives as they will vary depending on your job, but here are some examples of typical performance objectives that you might expect your workteam to achieve:

- receiving a maximum of two customer complaints each year;
- producing one new product idea every two years;
- meeting sales targets every three calendar months.

You may have noticed that all our examples of objectives contain performance standards that tell us 'how many', or 'how often', or 'by when'. Standards are usually expressed quantitatively, and refer to such measures as attendance, production rates and manufacturing tolerances. This means that performance is easily measured and the employee who is being appraised is able to monitor his or her improvement, so increasing his or her motivation.

There are many different ways in which people can be helped to improve their work performance. You might for example be able to help them to:

EXTENSION I
In the book *Effective Performance Appraisals* Robert Maddux discusses the topic – what is meant by goals and standards.

- increase productivity;
- decrease wastage;
- improve punctuality;
- deal more quickly with correspondence that arrives on their desk.

Activity 8 · 4 mins

Think about the members of your own workteam and some improvements you would like to see in its performance. Make a note of at least **three** things you would need to know before you could suggest improving performance. For example, before suggesting that it increases its work output you would need to know what its present workload is.

_____

_____

_____

_____

_____

You may have suggested that you would need the following information:

- what the measure of good performance is (i.e. the performance standard);
- what existing performance is, or was in the past;
- the nature of the workteam's strengths and weaknesses;
- what it can do to improve its performance;
- what help is available, for example, training.

You can learn more about setting performance objectives in _Motivating People_.

6.2 Assessing past performance and improving future performance

One of the best ways of improving your current and future performance at work is to learn from the recent past.

In many jobs performance objectives are very clear. For example, the objective to increase retail sales by 10 per cent over the same period as last year is clear and quantifiable.

However, in other jobs it is not clear what constitutes a satisfactory or good performance. Therefore it is essential to establish what is considered satisfactory or good performance and to gather evidence about past performance. This enables you to discuss this performance with the individual and to give feedback on the tasks that are completed well. It also makes it possible for you and the employee jointly to identify areas for improvement and to plan for the future.

6.3 Assessing training and development needs

One of the main objectives of any appraisal scheme is to focus on an employee's strengths and weaknesses, so that strengths can be highlighted and weaknesses can be remedied. Appraisal should be at the centre of training and development, giving increased understanding of the appraisee's performance.

Effective appraisal should accurately diagnose the learning needs of the appraisee, so that an effective training programme can be established.

Activity 9 · 3 mins

What makes a training programme effective? Write down **two** characteristics you think it should have, in order to be effective. Here is one to get you started.

It should be related to the job needs of the employee.

_____

_____

_____

_____

_____

_____

_____

_____

Your ideas will probably to similar to these.

- It should be related to the job needs of the employee.
- It should be related to the needs of the workplace.
- It should be designed with the support of management and the employee concerned.
- It should be realistic.

We are not suggesting that it is an easy task for two people to sit down and agree learning needs. There are many obstacles in the way of reaching agreement.

Activity 10 · 2 mins

Write down **one** reason why it may be difficult for employees to agree what their learning needs are with their manager.

_____

_____

You might have suggested one of the following 'obstacles'.

- They may not want to admit to weaknesses or shortcomings in their performance.
- They may become defensive if their manager mentions any weaknesses or shortcomings.
- They may not trust their manager's judgement.
- They may disagree over the different priorities.

Even though these obstacles may exist, organizations can sometimes find ways around them by, for example, training appraisers and appraisees, giving ongoing guidance and counselling, and using more objective appraisal techniques.

In Session B we will look in more detail at ways in which you can highlight and meet employees' identified training and development needs.

6.4 Assessing future potential

Organizations have to find staff to fill both short-term and long-term vacancies. Filling these vacancies may involve:

■ finding staff to do a new job;
■ finding staff to do an existing job.

The staff who fill these vacancies may be:

■ promoted from within the organization;
■ obtained from outside the organization.

Vacancies occur within organizations for a number of reasons. Here are some of the main reasons for vacancies occurring:

■ staff leaving;
■ maternity leave;
■ secondments;
■ retirements;
■ internal transfers;
■ promotions;
■ re-organization;
■ expansion.

An organization spends a lot of time planning its future direction and the use of its resources, including capital and equipment. It cannot do this properly without considering, at the same time, the future use of its most valuable resource – its employees.

Once the potential of different employees in an organization is identified, the supervisors and management must help them to realize it. If they don't, staff may lose heart and lose interest in what they are doing.

Activity 11 ·

3 mins

Think about your future plans for your own workteam. Write down **two** ways in which you can help its members to realize their potential.

_____

_____

_____

_____

There are clearly many ways in which this can be achieved. Here are five of them:

- discussion and agreement with you;
- planned work experience or secondment;
- attendance on training courses;
- completion of assignments;
- completion of projects.

One of the major benefits of performance appraisal is that employees are likely to gain motivation and job satisfaction if they feel that their capabilities, inclinations and personal needs are being satisfied at work.

6.5 Determining salary

In some organizations there is a clear link between performance and pay, and the appraisal process is used to assist in determining salary. There are arguments for and against performance-related pay (PRP). For example, many organizations claim that PRP results in better performance from managers and gains more commitment from them in achieving business objectives. Other organizations claim that it is not helpful to workteam building, and that individual employees are reluctant to discuss possible weaknesses when this may have a detrimental effect on any pay increase they may receive.

Activity 12 · 4 mins

Sharing out the money in organizations by giving pay rises often leads to conflict and difficulties. Write down **two** reasons why you think this is likely to happen.

_____

_____

_____

_____

Here are some common reasons.

- Employees often question the judgement of individual supervisors and first line managers.
- Employees believe that those who make the decisions are not in the best position to judge their performances and worth.
- Some employees may consider that they work harder than others and, therefore, deserve more money.
- Employees may believe that one incident around the time of appraisal has unfairly influenced the salary increase.
- Employees tend to compare each other's pay rises.

Organizations continually seek salary review procedures which are just and fair because they are aware that employees who are dissatisfied with salary levels are less likely to perform well.

Activity 13 · 3 mins

Write down **two** ways in which organizations can attempt to make their salary system just and fair.

_____

_____

_____

_____

There are many ways in which organizations can do this. Here are a few common methods:

- by using an effective appraisal system;
- by seeking staff views on the salary system;
- by looking at salary structures and systems in other organizations, perhaps in competing companies;
- by attempting to establish formulae and rules to determine salary increases.

Many companies use consultants to help them establish improved salary review systems. These consultants carry out job evaluations to look at the relative demands of jobs within an organization. This is to provide a base for relating differences in pay to the different requirements of the jobs.

If appraisal is to be used to make salary review decisions, first line managers require relevant and objective information to determine how well staff have performed over a period of time.

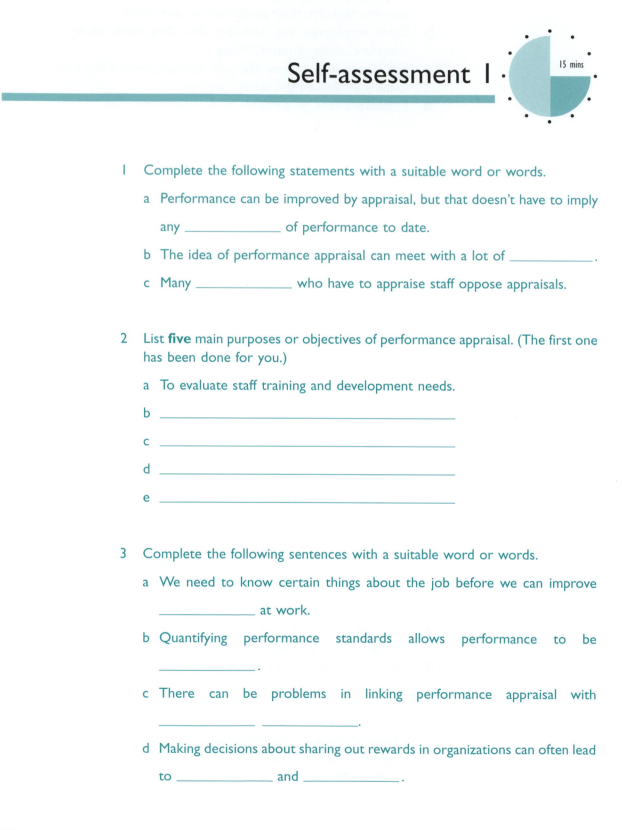

Self-assessment 1 · 15 mins

1 Complete the following statements with a suitable word or words.

a Performance can be improved by appraisal, but that doesn't have to imply any _____ of performance to date.

b The idea of performance appraisal can meet with a lot of _____ .

c Many _____ who have to appraise staff oppose appraisals.

2 List **five** main purposes or objectives of performance appraisal. (The first one has been done for you.)

a To evaluate staff training and development needs.

b _____

c _____

d _____

e _____

3 Complete the following sentences with a suitable word or words.

a We need to know certain things about the job before we can improve _____ at work.

b Quantifying performance standards allows performance to be _____ .

c There can be problems in linking performance appraisal with _____ _____ .

d Making decisions about sharing out rewards in organizations can often lead to _____ and _____ .

e A good salary review system should attempt to be _____

and _____ .

4 How can an organization ensure that it makes its system of adjusting salaries fair and just?

_____

_____

_____

Answers to these questions can be found on page 87.

7 Summary

- A definition of **performance appraisal** is:

'any procedure which helps the collecting, sharing, giving and using of information collected from and about people at work for the purposes of adding to their performance at work'.

- The **benefits** of performance appraisal are that it gives an opportunity to:

  - discuss an individual's performance at work;
  - give positive feedback to an individual;
  - identify any training needs the individual may have;
  - produce a record of the individual's performance at work;
  - negotiate and agree work targets and objectives;
  - identify any weaknesses, and look for ways in which performance at work can be improved;
  - clarify roles;
  - discuss the job.

- **Resistance** to performance appraisal can be overcome on two fronts.

  a Organizations can make sure that:
    - their first line managers are well trained to run appraisals;
    - there is a right of appeal;
    - paperwork systems are kept to a minimum.

  b First line managers can make sure that:
    - appraisal is an ongoing process;
    - they plan and prepare for interviews;
    - they overcome any prejudice or bias they may have;
    - they build up trust with the people who work for them;
    - they use objective standards;
    - they give only constructive criticism.

- The main **aims and objectives** of appraisal are:

  - setting performance objectives;
  - assessing past and current performance;
  - improving current and future performance;
  - assessing training and development needs;
  - determining salary levels;
  - developing individuals;
  - assessing future potential;
  - improving motivation;
  - providing job satisfaction.

Session B
The appraisal process

1 Introduction

There are many kinds and varieties of performance appraisal system and yet all systems should have a number of common components if they are to be considered as quality systems.

One quality requirement is that there should be careful planning and preparation for any appraisal interview that is held. This should happen for both the first line manager and the employee. Many organizations assist employees to prepare for the interview by providing them with a pre-appraisal form to complete. This gives them time to think through the past year and to plan what they would like to discuss. It also ensures that they are not 'put on the spot' when asked searching questions by their first line manager.

Performance appraisal systems should also ensure that the appraiser collects and considers information and data that has been collected over a period of time, i.e. since the last appraisal was carried out. Although most appraisals culminate in an interview it is the information that has been gathered over time that is discussed and forms the core of the process.

It is also essential that the results of performance appraisal be recorded. A variety of systems could be used, but they should all ensure that employees have a plan for the future that they are committed to and are motivated by.

2 Planning and preparation

Before any type of interview takes place, whether the purpose be selection, appraisal or discipline, the person conducting the interview must ensure that he or she plans and prepares thoroughly.

Activity 14

5 mins

Imagine you are about to conduct a performance appraisal interview. What things will you need to plan and prepare for? Write your thoughts down in the space provided below.

_____

_____

_____

_____

_____

_____

The first thing you will need to be clear about is what is to be achieved in the interview. To help decide on this you may need to start by looking at what was said at the last appraisal, and perhaps complete some draft comments on an appraisal form for this year. Of course, to decide what to say on this occasion, you will need to collect evidence of present performance, and perhaps talk to other people who will have a valid view on the employee's performance. In addition to this you will need to carry out some simple tasks such as:

- agreeing a date and time for the interview with the employee;
- briefing the employee;
- booking a room for the interview;
- ensuring that there will be no interruptions.

In addition to making sure that you plan and prepare thoroughly, it is important to allow time and the facilities for the employee to go through the same process. There are two main ways in which you can ensure that this happens. This is through:

■ briefing prior to the appraisal;
■ encouraging the employee to complete a pre-appraisal form (see 2.2 Pre-appraisal forms below).

2.1 Appraisal briefings

An appraisal briefing is a meeting between you and the person who is to be appraised. It should take place about one to two weeks before the actual appraisal interview. It should be an informal and fairly short meeting.

Activity 15 · 5 mins

In your opinion what should be achieved in an appraisal briefing?

_____

_____

_____

_____

_____

_____

A performance appraisal briefing should:

■ agree the date and time for the actual appraisal interview;
■ inform the employee of approximately how long the interview will last;
■ explain the purpose of the interview;
■ introduce the general topic areas that will be discussed;
■ invite the employee to add items to the agenda for discussion;
■ set his or her mind at rest;
■ allow him or her to ask any questions;
■ issue and explain the purpose of a pre-appraisal form.

2.2 Pre-appraisal forms

These forms are usually identical or very similar to the form that you will complete during the actual interview. They show the employee the questions that will be asked and the topics that will be covered.

A pre-appraisal form allows employees to plan answers to questions before the actual interview. For example, they can think about what their strengths and weaknesses are, and record examples on the form.

Allowing employees to prepare for an appraisal interview enables them to contribute well during discussions and ensures that the process is a pleasant one for them and not an ordeal.

3 Assessing performance

There are two stages to the process of assessing performance:

stage 1:   gathering information about the appraisee
stage 2:   the appraisal interview.

The remainder of this session looks at the tasks involved in stage 1.

Stage 2 is discussed in Session C – The Appraisal Interview.

3.1 Stage 1: Gathering information

Before you can hold the appraisal interview, you need to find out all you can about the employee in the work context.

Activity 16

2 mins

Suggest two types of information that will be useful to you when you carry out the appraisal interview.

_____

_____

_____

_____

Your suggestions might have included finding out about the employee's personal qualities and attitude to work, and his or her skill in carrying out specific tasks.

3.2 Assessing personal qualities

Early appraisal systems often concentrated totally on the attributes of the **person**. First line managers were required to comment on employees' personal characteristics. An example of such a system is shown on page 26.

More recent appraisal systems have moved away from this approach because of the difficulties associated with it, but first line managers are still frequently asked to comment on and evaluate personal characteristics.

Personal Qualities Appraisal Form	1	2	3	4	5	6
Performance (output and quality)						
Relations with colleagues and others						
Powers of expression						
Initiative						
Judgement						
Original thought						
Reaction to pressure						
Powers of leadership						
Ability to delegate, co-ordinate and direct						
Development of subordinates						

Overall rating [ ]   Month [   ]   Year [   ]

General comments:

Definitions:
1 Excellent
2 More than fully meets the standard for the position
3 Fully meets the standard for the position
4 Not fully up to standard required
5 Generally unsatisfactory
6 Unsatisfactory in all job aspects

Activity 17 · 15 mins

S/NVQ C12.2

This Activity may provide the basis of appropriate evidence for your S/NVQ portfolio. If you are intending to take this course of action, it might be better to write your answers on separate sheets of paper.

Look at the example of the Personal Qualities Appraisal Form again and complete it for one of your workteam. Having completed it, make a note of some of the difficulties you came across, or objections that you had to using this form for performance appraisal.

_____

_____

_____

_____

_____

_____

Perhaps the difficulties you thought you would have are among the following:

- It does not put any emphasis on the job itself.
- Not all the characteristics you are appraising are relevant to the job. How relevant is 'original thought' for instance, in your workteam?
- It does not put any emphasis on performance.
- It is difficult to measure personal characteristics and it may be difficult to keep likes and dislikes out of your thinking.
- A personal characteristic may be considered to be a strength by one first line manager and a weakness by another.

Because this type of appraisal is based on personality traits, it is often called:

a traits-orientated approach.

Performance appraisal needs to be about performance, measured in terms of results. More recent appraisal systems have therefore tended to take:

a results-orientated approach.

3.3 Assessing job skills

Performance should be measured in terms of results

There are a variety of techniques which can be used to assess performance but they should all compare actual performance against any performance standards or objectives set. One of your tasks as an appraiser is to ensure that evidence is gathered before the actual appraisal interview through techniques such as:

■ observing the employee;
■ examining examples of the work carried out by the employee;
■ talking to others about the employee;
■ talking directly to the employee.

This will enable you to build up an objective picture over a period of time about the work performance of the employee. You can then take this objective picture and evidence into the interview with you.

Observing the employee

As a first line manager you will come into contact with members of your workteam on a regular basis. You will be able to observe them carrying out jobs that you have given them. This observation can take place in passing or when you stop to check how well they are doing. You may not be conscious at the time that you are observing them but you may be able to give an opinion based on these informal observations at a later date.

You may also choose to organize some more formal performance observations. These will be planned, and your workteam member will be briefed about what is to happen.

When observing employees in a more formal environment it is important that you:

■ be as unobtrusive as possible;
■ allow the employee to complete tasks in the normal work environment;
■ complete all required training before the observation takes place.

Activity 18 · 6 mins

S/NVQ C12.2

This Activity may provide the basis of appropriate evidence for your S/NVQ portfolio. If you are intending to take this course of action, it might be better to write your answers on separate sheets of paper.

Give **one** example of when you have observed, either formally or informally, one of your workteam carrying out a task. Complete the form below giving details of the requested information.

Workteam member:
Details of task observed:
Timing details:
Performance standards used:

Examining examples of the work carried out by the employee

For some types of work it is essential to examine a finished piece of work. Sometimes the method of achieving the work is not so important – it is the standard of the result that matters. So you do not need to spend time observing methods of work but can examine completed items only.

To ensure objective assessment you need to:

- examine a number of similar products;
- establish the start and finish time of work – this is important if the time taken to complete a task is part of the performance standard;
- compare the finished product/service against the required standards.

Activity 19 · 5 mins

S/NVQ C12.2

This Activity may provide the basis of appropriate evidence for your S/NVQ portfolio. If you are intending to take this course of action, it might be better to write your answers on separate sheets of paper.

Give **two** instances of work you have examined in order to form an opinion about the standards of performance of members of your workteam.

Example 1	
Details of work examined:	Performance standards used:

Example 2	
Details of work examined:	Performance standards used:

4 Choosing the appraiser

Most appraisals are carried out by the employee's line manager. This is because the immediate line manager usually has the most relevant knowledge of the employee's job and is fully aware of how well the tasks that make up the job have been done.

However, not all schemes depend just upon the assessment by the immediate manager.

Appraisal by the immediate line manager is often called appraisal by 'father' and appraisal by the line manager's own manager is known as the 'grandfather' approach.

The **grandfather approach** has a number of advantages.

■ **It ensures fairness**

You cannot be certain that any system is absolutely fair, but the grandfather approach ensures, as far as possible, that any personal animosity between the appraisee and his or her immediate manager is not reflected in the appraisal.

■ **It provides an overview**

Grandfathers probably carry out appraisals for a number of people in different workteams and departments. They are therefore better placed than the immediate manager to make comparisons between staff in one department and another, and to see possible scope for development for the appraisee in another department. Unfortunately they also have less contact than the first line manager does with the person being assessed. In the same way, a grandparent has a broader view of what the grandchildren are doing and of their relative successes, failures, happiness and frustration, than the parents, who are much more deeply involved on a day-to-day basis.

■ **It maintains standards of assessment**

A grandfather figure, carrying out appraisals across a number of departments, is likely to apply the same standards throughout.

■ **It gives a second opinion**

In the same way as grandparents may see events within the family quite differently from parents, so a grandfather figure may form an independent view of the appraisee's performance. This may or may not support the immediate manager's assessment.

■ It provides a different company view

An appraisal should be a two-way process which gives the appraisee the opportunity to ask some questions about the organization and his or her role in its future. A grandfather figure should be in a better position to provide this sort of information and may give the person being interviewed a valuable insight into what is happening in the workplace.

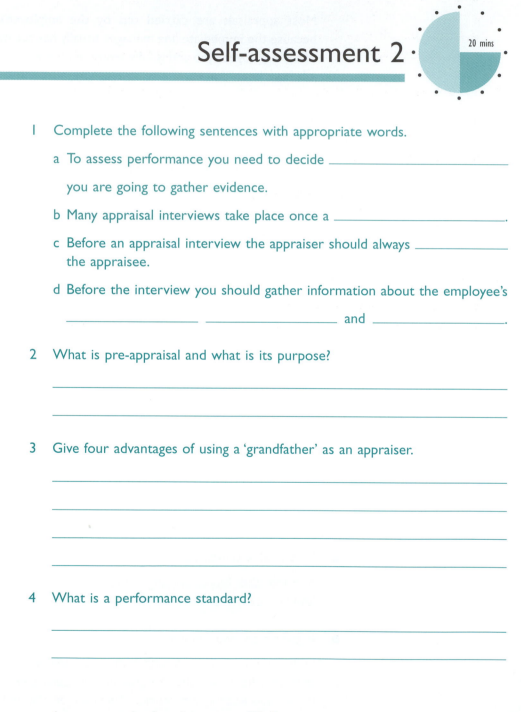

Self-assessment 2

20 mins

1 Complete the following sentences with appropriate words.

a To assess performance you need to decide _____

you are going to gather evidence.

b Many appraisal interviews take place once a _____.

c Before an appraisal interview the appraiser should always _____

the appraisee.

d Before the interview you should gather information about the employee's

_____ _____ and _____.

2 What is pre-appraisal and what is its purpose?

_____

_____

3 Give four advantages of using a 'grandfather' as an appraiser.

_____

_____

_____

_____

4 What is a performance standard?

_____

_____

Answers can be found on pages 87–8.

5 Summary

- When **planning and preparing** the first line manager should:
  - decide on interview aims;
  - collect evidence of present performance;
  - agree a date and time for the interview with the employee;
  - brief the employee;
  - book a room for the interview;
  - ensure that there will be no interruptions;
  - encourage the employee to complete a pre-appraisal form.

- **Before assessing performance** it will be necessary to decide upon:
  - the overall purpose of the job;
  - the key areas of the job;
  - the performance objectives.

- The two different **ways of assessing** are:
  - assessing personal qualities (traits orientated);
  - assessing job skills (results orientated).

- Different **methods of assessment** are:
  - observing the workteam member;
  - examining examples of work carried out by the workteam member.

Session C
The appraisal interview

1 Introduction

In Session B we looked at some techniques for ensuring that a structure exists within the appraisal process. We looked at the need to plan and prepare before the final interview actually takes place. This was stage 1 of the appraisal process, which included domestic issues like ensuring that a room was available, but also included ensuring that sufficient evidence had been gathered about the employee's performance over a period of time.

Session B also stated the importance of looking back and looking forward. This means that past performance must be reviewed and future performance planned for.

Even with all the necessary procedures in place, however, there is no guarantee that the appraisal interview will achieve its objectives. The best system will fail if the person operating it doesn't have the necessary skills.

In this session we will look at stage 2 of the appraisal process, the appraisal interview, beginning with an examination of the skills that you need to conduct an effective interview that results in the improvement of the employee's performance. You should also possess the skills to ensure that at the end of the interview the employee is left feeling positive and motivated to improve. Performance appraisal interviews are something that employees should look forward to, not dread.

2 Before the interview

Before the interview starts you must make sure that you have:

■ collected all the relevant information required during the interview;
■ set objectives for the interview and clarified these with the employee;
■ decided on the timing of the appraisal. Some organizations carry out appraisals on the anniversary of the employee's joining the company, or carry out all the staff appraisals in a relatively short space of time each year to coincide with the development of the company plan. A new employee may have more frequent appraisals, perhaps three-monthly, decreasing to yearly as performance improves;
■ allowed enough time. The appraisal interview needs adequate time to be productive and to ensure that the primary goals are achieved. There is no ideal figure for the duration of an appraisal interview but is it difficult to imagine the main objectives of an appraisal system being achieved in less than an hour.

Activity 20

3 mins

Suppose you plan to carry out two appraisal interviews in a day and your diary looks like this. Where would you fit in the appraisal interviews, given that each actual interview should last about an hour?

8.00	
8.30	*Development Group meeting (about an hour)*
9.00	
9.30 9.45	*Visiting supplier (not more than 30 minutes)*
10.00	
11.00	
12.00	
12.30	*Promised to have lunch with a colleague if possible*
1.00	
1.30	*Heads of Sections meeting with manager*
2.00	
2.30	*European Market (presentation to managers, might take one and a half hours)*
3.00	
4.00	
5.00	*Staff normally finish*

You would probably have to do one in the morning, at say 10.30 a.m. when the supplier had gone, and the other in the afternoon at 4.00 p.m. You shouldn't try to squeeze two into the morning, although, at a pinch, you might have a couple of hours free.

Of course, you might reasonably have decided to rearrange your other appointments and leave a whole day or half day as free as possible, in case the interviews take longer than anticipated. Certainly a high priority needs to be given to them.

You will need to make sure that you will not be interrupted by:

- telephone calls;
- the unexpected arrival of a visitor;
- other staff;
- a written message being passed to you.

You will also need to:

- ask the employee to arrange not to be interrupted;
- agree approximately how long you expect the interview to take.

It is important to ensure that the venue allows the appraisal interview to be carried out in a relaxed, friendly and supportive atmosphere. Even though we may not all have access to well-equipped interview rooms, there are several ways in which this kind of atmosphere can be created.

Activity 21 · 2 mins

Write down **two** ways in which you could achieve a relaxed, friendly and supportive atmosphere.

_____

_____

_____

_____

_____

Here are some suggestions.

- Use a neutral venue – the employee is immediately at a disadvantage if the interview is on your 'territory' with you in a dominant position.
- Use comfortable chairs – a relaxed, informal atmosphere is more easily established if you are both sitting in easy chairs rather than perched on upright ones.
- Come out from behind your desk – if you want to talk to each other on a friendly, equal basis, you should be sitting together without any barriers between you.
- And finally, as we have already said, make sure there are no interruptions.

3 At the start of the interview

If you are properly prepared then you can approach the actual appraisal interview feeling confident that it will be effective.

There are no hard-and-fast rules on conducting an appraisal interview, but you might find it helpful to bear the following points in mind.

3.1 Re-establish the objectives

It is important that you be clear about your objectives for the interview, and equally important that the employee should know and agree with these objectives.

If you look back to Session A you will see that there can be quite a few objectives that you may wish to achieve during the appraisal process:

- assessing past and current performance;
- setting performance objectives;
- improving current and future performance;
- assessing training and development needs;
- determining salary levels;
- developing individuals;
- assessing future potential;
- improving motivation;
- providing job satisfaction.

It wouldn't be very helpful if your main objective were to inform employees of a salary increase, but they were expecting to discuss training and development plans for the future.

Looking back at the list of objectives for appraisal we can agree that its two main purposes are:

- to assess current performance;
- to identify ways of improving future performance.

Whatever other objectives may be discussed in any particular appraisal interview, these two key objectives must be covered.

3.2 Choose an interview style

When deciding on what interview style to use you need to consider what your normal interview style is and the type of interview you will be conducting. During an appraisal interview it is important for your style to be one that encourages the employee to talk and allows you to listen.

Activity 22 · 5 mins

Examine these interviewing style options.

- The **tell** option

  In this option you tell the employees what their strengths and weaknesses are and inform them of the actions that need to be taken in order to improve.

- The **tell** and **sell** option

  Here you tell the employees what their strengths and weaknesses are but also give an explanation as to why you have that opinion. When you explain what actions need to taken in the future in order to improve you also sell the benefits to the employees.

■ The **tell** and **listen** option

In this option you again explain your own views on strengths, weaknesses and improvement action needed. However, after having explained your own point of view you allow the employees to express their own opinions too.

■ The **consultation** option

Here you first encourage the employees to explain their own views about strengths, weaknesses and improvement action needed. Having listened to what the employees have to say you decide exactly what action will take place.

■ The **joint problem-solving** option

In this option you and the employees work together to identify strengths, weakness and improvement actions required. The employees are encouraged to recommend solutions to any problems that are identified.

Which option is the one that you would choose when running an appraisal interview?

What do you consider the benefits of your chosen option to be?

_____

_____

_____

_____

_____

_____

_____

_____

Answers to this Activity can be found on page 89.

3.3 Keeping notes

You should explain to the employee that you are going to keep notes during the interview.

Activity 23 · 12 mins

What do you think is the main advantage of keeping notes during an appraisal interview?

_____

_____

_____

The advantage is that you will have a record of the main points of the interview, such as any concerns that the employee may have, new performance objectives and ideas for further training. This can then be used as a basis for discussion at the next performance review.

However, it is important to remember that the process of note-taking should not be allowed to dominate the interview.

4 During the interview

In this section we will consider a number of different skills that you will need to use during the appraisal interview. The first skill we will look at is that of encouraging the employee to talk.

4.1 Encourage the employee to talk

EXTENSION 2
The video _How Am I Doing?_ produced by Video Arts examines ways of identifying problems and opportunities during an appraisal interview. It also shows how to agree and review a plan of action.

It is important that you allow the employee to talk early on in the interview. This is so that the individual's point of view is incorporated in any conclusions drawn on his or her performance.

If the first line manager has chosen the right interview style there will be trust and openness during the interview. A warm and friendly manner will also encourage the employee to talk.

Activity 24 · 2 mins

Angela has worked at Myrestone for nearly twelve months and Joan Webster, her first line manager, has informed her that her first appraisal interview is due in two weeks' time. Before the interview Joan Webster had written down her views of Angela's performance over the last twelve months. Joan has always thought that Angela is one of the best employees she had ever employed.

Under the heading 'punctuality' in the appraisal report she had given a 'very poor' rating, because for the last four Mondays Angela has arrived at work up to fifteen minutes late.

Can you think of a possible reason for Angela's recent poor timekeeping?

_____

_____

_____

_____

_____

_____

_____

There may be several possible reasons, including perhaps that Angela is just becoming a poor timekeeper.

However, the real reason is that Angela's mother was an out-patient at the local hospital and was attending it for four consecutive Mondays. Angela drove her mother to the hospital and on three occasions the doctor was twenty minutes late in seeing her mother. This resulted in Angela being late for work.

Learning this at the interview, Joan Webster changed her rating to 'very good'.

The way in which you can encourage an employee to talk is by asking the right type of questions.

It is also important for you to give the employees the opportunity to comment on and assess their own work. This can be done through:

- **Pre- or self-appraisal systems**

  We covered this type of system in our section on planning and preparation and stated that it allowed employees to give some thought to their own strengths and weaknesses before the appraisal interview. This allows them to be able to answer any questions put to them by you and to state their own views and opinions clearly.

  You should always ensure that the employee has had sufficient time to complete this part of the appraisal.

- **Questions during the interview**

  During the interview you should encourage employees to state their own views and opinions on the work they have carried out. You should encourage them to give specific details of work carried out and should fully explore all work issues raised.

Activity 25 · 5 mins

S/NVQs C12.2, C12.3

This Activity may provide the basis of appropriate evidence for your S/NVQ portfolio. If you are intending to take this course of action, it might be better to write your answers on separate sheets of paper.

Give some details below of an occasion during the performance appraisal process when you gave an individual from your workteam the opportunity to assess his or her own work. (You may not be able to complete this activity if you have not yet carried out an appraisal.)

If you are compiling an S/NVQ portfolio it may be useful to ask the individual concerned to countersign your account of the occasion. This account may then form the basis of acceptable evidence.

_____

_____

_____

_____

_____

4.2 Ask questions

There are some questions where it is impossible for an employee to answer just Yes or No. These questions require them to give some information about their job or the way in which it is carried out. They require the employee to join in a discussion. These questions are called **open** questions.

Open questions usually start with the words:

- What?
- Where?
- Why?
- Who?
- When?
- How?

Activity 26

5 mins

Think of a member of your workteam who will soon be interviewed by you as part of the appraisal process. Write down some open questions that you would like to ask. Try and think of at least **five** different questions.

_____

_____

_____

_____

_____

_____

_____

_____

_____

It may be that an open question prompts some information from your workteam member, but not in sufficient detail for appraisal purposes. It may then be necessary for you to probe a little deeper for some more information. This can be achieved by the using the following methods:

- asking a follow-up question like 'Could you give me a specific example of that?';
- giving a verbal prompt using a variety of short sounds like 'Humm' or 'Ah ha' or even using silence to encourage the employee to say more;
- encouraging the employee to continue by using phrases like 'Really?' or 'Tell me more';
- repeating a key phrase from what the employee has just said, for example:

Employee:	**'That's the way it's always been.'**
First line manager:	**'Always been?'**
Employee:	**'Well certainly since last year when we …'**

It is important for you to listen to the employees. If they feel that they have been encouraged to give their own views, and that you are listening to them with an open mind, their performance is more likely to improve.

4.3 Listen

EXTENSION 3
The Dreaded Appraisal is a Video Arts video which has key points on how to ask open questions and listen actively.

There is a well-known saying that 'The reason we have two ears and one mouth is so that we may listen more and talk less.' This saying is very relevant to an appraisal interview.

Your job in an appraisal interview is to ask sufficient questions to encourage and permit employees to talk openly and fully about their work. Having stimulated them to talk you should then **listen!**

Activity 27 · 4 mins

How good are you at listening? Complete the questionnaire below and rate your listening skills.

	Never	Sometimes	Always
1 I am easily distracted.			
2 I listen selectively.			
3 I get bored while others are talking.			
4 I finish other people's sentences.			
5 I interrupt other people.			
6 I maintain eye contact.			
7 I check understanding if unsure.			
8 I summarize other people's comments.			
9 I am interested in what people have to say.			
10 I am relaxed during interviews.			

Hopefully in answer to questions 1–5 you stated that you never do these things, and in answer to questions 6–10 you that you always do these things. If your answers differed in any way give some thought to how you can change your behaviour.

Why is it that people find listening so difficult? There are a number of reasons for this and we have included some of them below.

Managers have difficulty listening to others when:

- the views the other person holds are different from their own;
- they are being told something they do not want to hear;
- the other person speaks in long sentences;
- they start to plan what they are going to say next, even before the other person has finished talking;
- the other person has an accent or dialect;

■ the interview environment is noisy;
■ they dislike the person;
■ they are tired or under stress.

Not only is it important for you to listen effectively to what the employee is saying during the appraisal interview, it is also important to be seen to listen. The use of appropriate body language such as eye contact, smiling and nodding your head can be very useful here.

4.4 Give effective feedback

We all like to know how we are doing and how others see us. The purpose of feedback therefore is to offer information about the effect of a person's behaviour or performance. It should start a process that leads to development and change, and works best where the relationship between the giver and the receiver is already open, honest and respectful.

Feedback can be positive or negative

If given in a positive way, feedback is usually helpful in pointing out ways in which the job could have been done better, more quickly or more in line with the organization's requirements. Praise can be valuable in giving people a glow of satisfaction which makes all their hard work worthwhile. Thoughtless or harsh criticism on the other hand, can be very damaging; many people will respond by doing even less work, or taking less care.

If it is to be positive, feedback must:

■ be obviously offered for the receiver's benefit;
■ leave the receiver free to decide what to do with the information given;
■ imply an equal relationship between giver and receiver;
■ not be judgemental;
■ be expressed through 'I' statements (for example 'I thought that you found that task difficult').

We all find it easier to tell someone how wonderful they are, but what about when we need to let them know there is room for improvement? Feedback is seen as negative criticism if it:

■ demands that the other person change;
■ arises within a hierarchy (for example a senior manager has stated that he wants to see a change of behaviour);
■ is judgemental;
■ includes 'you' statements, for example 'You speak too slowly'.

Many people's experience of receiving criticism is negative or even humiliating, but it can be a good experience if done constructively.

To give constructive criticism well, it helps if you:

- plan ahead – decide exactly what you want to say, and avoid snap judgements or comments about things that cannot be changed;
- say specifically what you think is going well;
- try to give twice as much positive information as negative;
- be selective about what you say and avoid dwelling on minor details;
- be specific about what you think could be improved;
- remember to only comment on what the person does, not who the person is;
- respect the person you are talking to;
- give facts, not opinions;
- state what changes you expect and help the employees to work out how they will achieve these.

Activity 28 · 5 mins

Think back over last week at work. Make a list of how often you have received or given feedback or constructive criticism from and to work colleagues. Was there any time in the week when you would have found it helpful or motivating to receive more positive feedback on something you had done?

_____

_____

_____

Now think of feedback you have received, either negative or positive. What effect did it have?

_____

_____

_____

It is quite likely that you received no feedback at all. Many people go for weeks without any comment on their work so they really have no idea whether they are doing well or badly. This can only contribute to a feeling of isolation – if there is no appreciation and no attempt to acknowledge difficulties, it is almost impossible for people to improve and quite difficult to even take pride in work.

Feedback can be informal or formal

Informal feedback should be given on a regular basis as part of your everyday job as a first line manager. The more quickly you give feedback to employees about their performance, the more likely it is to influence their future performance.

Activity 29 · 3 mins

How regularly do you provide feedback to the members of your team about their performance? How do you think they feel about this?

_____

_____

_____

_____

If you rarely give feedback your team members are likely to feel negative and resentful about it. Conversely, if they receive frequent feedback, as long as some of it is complimentary, they will probably feel quite positive about it.

While informal feedback should be immediate, formal feedback takes longer. This is because formal feedback is often derived from such sources as:

- information gathering prior to an employee's appraisal interview;
- management reports and charts;
- production figures;
- feedback from customers.

It is important for you to pass on any formal feedback to your team because this helps to maintain morale and makes it feel an integral part of the success of the project or organization.

Activity 30

4 mins

Apart from performance appraisals, what other sources of formal feedback do you have access to that you could usefully pass on to your team?

_____

_____

_____

Whatever the formal feedback that you receive yourself, try from now on to develop a regular routine for passing on to your team any items that would be useful in their work or that would increase their motivation.

5 Agreeing future performance

5.1 Agreeing improvements

Before the end of the appraisal interview you must come to an agreement with the employees in three key areas:

- areas where improved performance is required;
- what training they might need;
- what their future objectives are to be.

5.2 Identifying areas that need improvement

The aim of the discussions you have had during the interview is to identify areas where the employees could improve their performance. Such areas could relate to the way they do their job, their motivation or their attitude.

If both of you have been able to speak honestly and openly, the result should be a list of actions (including standards of performance) to be taken before the next appraisal. Some of these may require the acquisition of new skills or knowledge, and we will look at how this can be arranged next.

5.3 Identifying training and development needs

In Session A we agreed that effective appraisal should accurately diagnose the learning needs of employees. These needs may arise for many reasons. For example:

■ changed standards or targets in an existing job;
■ the introduction of new skills or tasks;
■ to bring performance up to the acceptable standard.

Whatever the reason, often the appraisal process will highlight a training or development need. This means that you will need to gather information about what the employee does now and what he or she should be able to do.

In order to do this you will first need to agree performance objectives for a future period. The performance standards in these objectives may be different from those the employee has just been appraised against and you will need to discuss the reasons for this. Once the new standards have been agreed you will then need to see if the employee will require any help in order to reach the new standards. The information gathered under the section on assessing performance can be used here.

EXTENSION 4
The topic of identifying and meeting training needs through the appraisal system is covered in the book *Managing People – A Competence Approach to Supervisory Management.*

Once information has been gathered about the training need you must then give some thought to the way in which the training need is to be met.

Methods of training may include the following:

■ On-the-job training

This type of training will take place in the employee's normal working environment. It may take the form of a demonstration, coaching, counselling, mentoring, etc.

■ Courses

These courses could be organized internally or externally to the organization but will take place away from the pressures of the employee's normal working environment. Courses will usually combine different training methods: talks, discussions, videos, practical exercises, etc.

- **Open and flexible learning**

  Flexible learning could include tutor-supported open learning programmes, computer-based learning or the use of interactive videos. It might also include other types of self-developmental activities such as multimedia training or reading.

- **Visits**

  First line managers may be able to arrange visits for employees to meet and discuss issues with both customers and suppliers. It may also be possible to arrange visits to conferences and exhibitions.

- **Projects**

  Training needs can also be met by allowing employees to take on special projects. This may require them to spend time in other departments or companies, gaining additional experience and knowledge.

Activity 31

6 mins

Think of a member of your workteam whose performance standards or targets you intend to change and who will need some additional training in order to meet the new standards you intend to set, and complete the form below.

Details of new objective or standard:
Training and development need(s) arising from the change:
Training method(s) to be used:

The important point is to make clear for both parties what action you agree for the future and to record it. You will learn about keeping records in Session D – Assessment reports and records.

5.4 Agreeing an action plan

The interview should be concluded by agreeing an action plan.

Activity 32 · 3 mins

Make a note of **two** things that you think an action plan should contain.

_____

_____

_____

_____

An action plan should contain:

- recommended future action;
- the individual's training and development needs;
- resources required;
- the period of time concerned, e.g. six months;
- performance targets.

The action plan on page 55 is a good example as it sets out clearly the training required and the performance objectives to be achieved. To be effective, however, it needs to be passed on to other people who can help put it into effect (the training manager, for instance), and it needs to be monitored.

Monitoring involves checking regularly to see that the training is taking place, that it is successful, and that it is as relevant and to the point as was intended.

Action Plan – John Wilson

1   Future action:

- to improve punctuality to at least 90 per cent;
- learn to log sales figures (manager to train during first week of July).

2   Development plan:

- to undertake ILM Certificate in First Line Management on afternoon release at college next September;
- to attend the next 'time management' course in the training room.

3   Resources:

- £300 to be allocated from training budget (TW to authorize).

4   Time period:

- six months.

5   Review:

- review John Wilson's performance in three calendar months.

Even if the appraisal system has a long preparation period and an effective appraisal interview, it can still fall into disrepute if the action recommended is not taken.

Activity 33

30 mins

S/NVQ C12.3

This Activity may provide the basis of appropriate evidence for your S/NVQ portfolio. If you are intending to take this course of action, it might be better to write your answers on separate sheets of paper.

Think of a recent action plan you may have drawn up for a member of your workteam. Complete the action plan provided below. If you have not recently drawn up a suitable action plan then this Activity can be used to draw one up.

Action Plan
Future action:
Development plan:
Resources:
Time period:
Review:

The advantage in recording future action in an action plan is that at the next performance appraisal interview this action can be used as the basis for discussion and for measuring the employee's performance.

5.5 Concluding the interview

It is important at this point to check that the notes you will have taken are clear and complete. You should also summarize what has been said while the employee is still with you, and fill in anything you have missed. In many organizations you would give a copy of what has been agreed to the employee.

6 After the interview

6.1 Monitoring future performance against objectives

Once the appraisal interview is over, there is a risk that everything will settle back to how it was before, because all change requires effort. Therefore, if you fail to follow up what has been agreed during the appraisal, the employee could become demotivated and cynical about the whole appraisal process, and you could lose credibility as a manager.

So it is important for you to monitor the employee's progress towards achieving the performance objectives that have been set at the interview.

Activity 34 · · 3 mins

What methods could you use to monitor how well the employee is progressing towards achieving the agreed objectives?

_____

_____

_____

_____

Your suggestions might have included:

- holding regular reviews (say, every three months) during which you would discuss the employee's progress and identify any problems that may prevent achievement of the objectives;
- encouraging the employee to give you frequent informal feedback on progress;
- regularly observing progress by 'walking about'.

Throughout the monitoring process, you should be prepared to respond to deviations from the action plan by:

- discussing any problems the employee is having, and identifying solutions such as providing additional resources, changing the working environment or acquiring additional information;
- involving the employee in clarifying or amending the performance standards;
- encouraging the employee to find his or her own solutions to the deviation;
- arranging further training;
- agreeing amendments to the plan if these appear necessary.

One of the most effective tools you have in helping employees to achieve their goals is to boost their confidence by providing immediate feedback and regularly praising achievement – however small this may be. There is nothing as effective in keeping people motivated as being told that they are doing a good job.

Self-assessment 3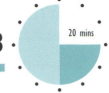

20 mins

1 What type of information do you think an appraiser may need to collect before conducting a performance appraisal interview?

_____

_____

_____

_____

2 Complete the following statements with a suitable word or words.

a Appraisers must ensure that they agree the _____ of an appraisal interview with the individual concerned.

b Appraisers must ensure that they collect _____ about the employee's performance.

c Appraisers should ensure there are no _____ .

3 Complete the following statements with a suitable word or words.

a If the appraiser is _____ _____ the appraisal interview will be more _____ .

b A first line manager carrying out an appraisal should encourage the employee to _____ .

c Both during and after the appraisal interview the employee expects _____ .

d Feedback should be _____ and _____ .

4 What should be included in an action plan? In the workbook we have mentioned five things.

_____

_____

_____

_____

_____

Answers to these questions can be found on page 88.

7 Summary

- **Before the interview** it is important to:

  - collect the relevant information
  - set the interview objectives
  - decide on the timing
  - make sure that are no interruptions
  - allow enough time.

- **At the start of the interview** you should remember to:

  - re-establish the objectives;
  - choose an interviewing style;
  - prepare to make brief notes.

- **During the interview** you should:

  - encourage the individual to talk;
  - ask questions;
  - listen;
  - give effective feedback.

- **Feedback** can be formal or informal, negative or positive.

- **Agreeing future performance** includes:

  - identifying areas that need improvement;
  - identifying training and development needs;
  - agreeing an action plan.

- After an appraisal interview it is vital that you **follow up and monitor** future performance.

Session D
Assessment reports and records

1 Introduction

In Session C we looked at the following topics:

- reviewing performance against existing performance objectives;
- assessing personal qualities;
- assessing job skills;
- setting new performance objectives;
- identifying training and development needs.

We considered how important it is for you to record such information during the appraisal interview so that it can be referred to again later, perhaps at the next appraisal interview.

In this session we are going to examine the choice of formats available for recording what has happened at the interview, and who should have access to such records.

2 Recording systems

There are three basic types or recording system. They are as follows:

- comparison with objectives;
- ratings;
- narrative reports.

2.1 Comparison with objectives

If specific performance objectives have been agreed on a previous occasion it is possible for the interview to be based around these objectives. The appraisal document can record the summary of achievements against the pre-set objectives and can also allow some space for comments.

This method of recording assessments is quite objective but needs to allow space for subjective comment about such things as reasons for objectives not having been met, specific examples, and so on.

Activity 35

20 mins

S/NVQ C12.3

This Activity may provide the basis of appropriate evidence for your S/NVQ portfolio. If you are intending to take this course of action, it might be better to write your answers on separate sheets of paper.

Here is an example of a form using objective comparison.

Performance Appraisal Document

Strictly Confidential

Name _____   Appraised by _____

Job title _____   Review period _____

Appraisal date _____

Objectives set	Targets set	Performance rating*	General comments

* 1 = Exceeded objectives and targets; 2 = Met objectives and targets; 3 = small shortfall in meeting objectives and targets; 4 = Significant shortfall in meeting objectives and targets.

In the 'Objectives set' column write down three performance objectives that you have recently set for one of your team. Don't forget to include performance standards. Then discuss the achievement of each objective with the individual and agree a performance rating. Write this rating in the third column on the form, and add any comments you may wish to make.

2.2 Ratings

Rating scores permit you to rate particular aspects of an employee's performance against some form of numerical or alphabetical score. The previous example with regard to objectives is one example of a rating but two more specific examples are given here.

Behaviourally anchored rating scales (BARS)

Using this recording system you are given a series of statements or questions about performance and has to rate the appraisee on a scale (e.g. of 1–6, or A–E where 1 and A = excellent and 6 and E = unacceptable) according to each statement.

Here is an example of a BARS

ABC Company (BARS)	
Customer service	Rating
1 Answers the phone immediately	1
2 Provides helpful advice to telephone customers	3
3 Always keeps cool with angry customers	1
4 Gives priority to telephone customers over direct callers	4
5 Usually answers correspondence within two days	2

Activity 36 · 3 mins

Given that the rating scale on the BARS is:

1	2	3	4	5	6
excellent	very good	above average	average	poor	very poor

which customer service behaviours could be improved by the person appraised?

Clearly this person shows considerable room for improvement in providing helpful advice on the telephone (3) and giving priority to telephone customers over direct callers (4). Some improvement could be made in dealing promptly with correspondence (2), although performance in that area is already very good.

Behavioural observation scale (BOS)

This is a slightly different way of linking behaviour and ratings. As the appraiser you are given a series of statements which describe behaviour in a number of areas of a job. You are then asked to assess the employee and to indicate on a scale (e.g. of 1–6, or A–E) the extent to which the employee displays the characteristic being looked at.

The example below shows the BARS example we looked at earlier, adapted so that it is presented as a behaviourial observation scale.

ABC Company (BOS)							
Customer service							
1 Answers the phone immediately							
Almost never	6	5	4	3	2	1	Almost always
2 Provides very helpful advice on the telephone							
Almost never	6	5	4	3	2	1	Almost always
3 Keeps cool with angry customers							
Almost never	6	5	4	3	2	1	Almost always
4 Gives equal consideration to both telephone callers and direct callers							
Almost never	6	5	4	3	2	1	Almost always
5 Answers correspondence within two days							
Almost never	6	5	4	3	2	1	Almost always

Activity 37 · ⏱ 5 mins

S/NVQ C12.2

This Activity may provide the basis of appropriate evidence for your S/NVQ portfolio. If you are intending to take this course of action, it might be better to write your answers on separate sheets of paper.

Probably some of the jobs of your workteam include an element of telephone use (although it may not tally exactly with the areas examined in the BOS example for Customer Service). Spend a minute or two trying to rate one of your workteam's telephone behaviour by circling the appropriate rating on the form.

Make a note of any difficulties you encountered when using this type of performance appraisal technique.

_____

_____

_____

_____

_____

You may have found the task quite difficult and time consuming. In this example we asked you to concentrate on only one element of a job. You would need a wide variety of forms to take everyone's job into account.

2.3 Narrative reports

This recording system allows you to express views and opinions in your own words. Usually the document gives headings to assist with subject areas. This method of recording information is usually used in conjunction with other recording methods.

Here is a typical example of the narrative section of an appraisal form.

Performance
Areas of job where performance is particularly good:
Areas of job where performance needs improving:

Activity 38 · 15 mins

S/NVQs C12.2, C12.3

This Activity may provide the basis of appropriate evidence for your S/NVQ portfolio. If you are intending to take this course of action, it might be better to write your answers on separate sheets of paper.

Complete the narrative report above for one of the members of your workteam. In the space below record any remarks you may have about this method of recording appraisal comments.

_____

_____

_____

_____

You may have found this method of recording comments very flexible, in that it allowed you to express yourself freely. However, you may feel that this system would make comparison between staff of different sections difficult due to the subjective nature of the comments made.

We have now looked in some detail at different types of appraisal system and the different situations in which they could be used. Unfortunately a good system on its own does not guarantee that the appraisal will be effective. For a good system to work well it requires the appraiser to have the right appraisal interview skills.

3 Who should have access to appraisal records?

3.1 Access by the appraiser

EXTENSION 5
An excellent video and workbook which will prove useful to first line managers in reviewing the skills covered in this workbook is *The Empowering Appraisal* produced by BBC for Business.

If an appraisal system is open the employees being appraised see their appraisal reports and perhaps even sign the completed appraisal report. On the other hand, with a closed appraisal system, the appraisal report is secret.

There are advantages and disadvantages with a closed system. These are as follows:

- Advantages of a closed system:

  - Appraisers may be more unguarded.
  - The organization may get a more frank assessment of its staff.
  - If appraisers give a poor assessment there may be less ultimate embarrassment.
  - There is less risk of souring the relationship between appraiser and appraisee.

- Disadvantages of a closed system:

  - Employees may be suspicious.
  - Appraisers can make judgements without the need to justify them.
  - The whole atmosphere of the department or organization may be affected.
  - It is more difficult for employees to improve their performance if the appraisal is kept secret.

What is more, since the Data Protection Acts of 1984 and 1998 employees have a right to see the assessment if appraisal records are computerized.

The trend appears to be towards more open appraisal, as this seems to strengthen employees' commitment to appraisal as a concept.

3.2 Access by others

There may or may not be clear guidelines within your organisation as to who, apart from the employees concerned, has a right to see their records. Those who have access rights might include:

■ the employees' departmental head;
■ the human resources department;
■ members of an Employment Tribunal (in the case of a future employment dispute).

It is important to keep in mind the protection given to employees' rights under the Data Protection Acts. For more information see the Super Series workbook *Managing Lawfully – People and Employment*.

Self-assessment 4

20 mins

1 In the 'comparison with objectives' recording system what two things are compared?

_____

2 What does BARS stand for?

_____

3 What does BOS stand for?

_____

4 Give three disadvantages of a closed appraisal system.

_____

_____

_____

Answers to these questions can be found on page 89.

4 Summary

- Three types of appraisal recording system are:
  - comparison with objectives;
  - ratings;
  - narrative reports.

- Appraisal systems may be open or closed.

- The Data Protection Acts give employees rights in regard to the records held about them.

Performance checks

1 Quick quiz

Jot down your answers to the following questions on *Appraising Performance*.

Question 1   When should first line managers assess the performance of their workteams?

_____

_____

Question 2   What more should an effective appraisal system be than one in which the first line manager particularly praises the good points of the employee being appraised?

_____

_____

Question 3   Should performance appraisal help workteam members to improve their future performance or act as a check on their past performance? Give a reason for your answer.

_____

_____

_____

Question 4   Why is it important for workteam members to know the standard they are achieving and what is expected of them?

_____

_____

_____

Question 5   When and how often should feedback be given to a workteam member about his or her work performance?

_____

_____

Question 6   Why should an effective appraisal system help an employee identify his or her training and development needs?

_____

_____

Question 7   What did early examples of appraisal systems concentrate on?

_____

_____

Question 8   What does the trait system of appraisal emphasize?

_____

_____

Question 9   What are the benefits of having an open system of appraisal?

_____

_____

Question 10   Who else, apart from the appraisee's superior, might be interested in the outcome of appraisal?

_____

_____

Question 11   Can the appraiser be effective if he or she knows nothing about the employee's job? Give a reason for your answer.

_____

_____

Question 12   How important is the atmosphere created during an appraisal interview?

_____

_____

Question 13   What part does preparation play in an effective appraisal interview?

_____

_____

Question 14   Fill in the gaps in the following sentences:

The purpose of feedback is to offer information about a person's

_____ and _____ .

The process of _____ should not be allowed to

_____ the appraisal interview.

Question 15   Suggest three methods you could use to monitor team
members' performance.

_____

_____

_____

Answers to these questions can be found on pages 90–1.

2 Workbook assessment

60 mins

Read the following case study incident and then deal with the questions that follow, writing your answers on a separate sheet of paper.

Your line manager learns that you have been studying the subject of appraisal as part of your self-development programme. She tells you that although she has to do appraisals for her 12 staff, she has always found it very time-consuming and difficult since her staff all react differently.

'It's like playing God,' she says, 'having to make a judgement of people which affects their future prospects and their salary levels.'

She asks you if you can spare an hour some time next week to talk to both her and the workteam and answer some questions about appraisal. Later on that day she gives you five questions she would like you to answer at next week's meeting.

1 What are the advantages to the appraiser of undertaking appraisal of staff?

2 What are the advantages to the employee of having an appraisal interview?

3 What things should be concentrated on in an appraisal: job performance, or personal qualities, or both?

4 How can the first line manager help the workteam prepare for the appraisal interview?

5 How can the first line manager follow up what has been agreed at the appraisal interview? Is this important?

3 Work-based assignment

60 mins

S/NVQs C12.2, C12.3

The time guide for this assignment gives you an approximate idea of how long it is likely to take you to write up your findings. You will need to spend some additional time gathering information, perhaps talking to colleagues and thinking about the assignment.

Your written response to this assignment may form the basis of evidence for your S/NVQ portfolio. The assignment is also designed to help you demonstrate your competence in:

■ planning and prioritizing;
■ managing and obtaining the commitment of others;
■ thinking and taking decisions.

What you have to do

1   Briefly describe the appraisal scheme which operates in your workplace. Enclose (if available) a copy of the appraisal documentation.

2   Evaluate your present appraisal system and suggest ways in which it could be improved. You could use the following headings for evaluation purposes:

  ■ Preparation and Pre-appraisal
  ■ Appraisal of Job Skills
  ■ Appraisal of Personal Qualities
  ■ Assessment of Potential
  ■ Setting of Objective Targets
  ■ Training and Development Needs
  ■ Action Planning
  ■ Appraisal Documentation

3   Present your ideas for change to your line manager. How will you gain commitment from him or her to your ideas?

If your organization does not have a formal appraisal scheme describe the sort of scheme you would like to see introduced and explain why you think your choice would be appropriate.

Reflect and review

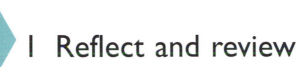

1 Reflect and review

Now that you have completed your work on *Appraising Performance*, let us review our workbook objectives.

You should be better able to:

- define performance appraisal, its aims, purposes and benefits.

  Performance appraisal can mean different things to different organizations and it's important that everyone be clear about what their organization sees as being performance appraisal. Therefore you need to clarify the following.

  - What does your organization aim to get out of performance appraisal?

    _____

    _____

  - What does it see as being the benefits of performance appraisal?

    _____

    _____

The next objective in this workbook was:

- to plan and prepare for a performance appraisal interview.

  We considered this subject in some depth in both Session B and Session C. No performance appraisal interview will run as well as it could if the first line manager has not planned and prepared before the interview. The preparation could take many forms.

Now we would like you to consider the following issues.

■ What methods will you use to collect evidence on the performance of the individual?

_____

_____

■ What will you include in your briefing to the individual?

_____

_____

■ Will you use a system of pre-appraisal?

_____

_____

■ Where will you run your appraisals and how long do you think they should last?

_____

_____

The third objective in the workbook was:

■ to agree performance objectives.

In the workbook we have tried to show you very clearly that it is essential that employees work to objective targets. This helps you review their past achievement and also helps to decide what is to be achieved in the future. Before you start setting objective targets for any of your workteam you should consider the following issues.

■ How will you inform workteam members of the required work standards?

_____

_____

■ How will you ensure that targets are jointly agreed?

_____

_____

The next objective was:

■ to make valid and reliable assessments.

In the workbook you learned that there are a number of steps you can take to ensure that your assessments are valid and reliable, including careful preparation and allowing appraisees to make a full contribution to the discussion. You should think about the following questions.

■ Do appraisees have enough opportunity at the moment to give an input into their appraisal?

_____

_____

■ How can you ensure in the future that the assessments you make are valid and reliable?

_____

_____

The next workbook objective was:

■ to assess the job skills and personal qualities of staff.

We have examined the benefits and problems of assessing both the job skills and personal qualities of your workteam. We found that assessing personal qualities alone would not provide you with the information that you will need in order to help your workteam improve. You should now give some thought to these questions.

■ Will you include the assessment of personal qualities in your appraisal system?

_____

_____

■ How will you assess job skills?

_____

_____

Another objective contained in the workbook was:

■ to identify training and development needs.

Appraisal is all about helping people at work to improve their performance. Once the areas for improvement have been identified, training and development is one of the main ways in which to achieve this improvement. Now think about the following.

■ What resources do you have available to you to meet training and development needs?

_____

_____

■ How will you ensure that the training needs identified are in line with the organization's business objectives?

_____

_____

Another objective we looked at in this workbook was:

■ to ask appropriate interview questions.

In order to review performance and plan for the future it is necessary to talk to the employee and gather information. This requires the first line manager to ask appropriate questions. We examined the use of open questions and how further information could be gathered through probing. As a result of this you might now like to think about the following issues.

■ How can you pre-prepare some interview questions?

_____

_____

■ At present how good are your questioning skills? How could you improve them?

_____

_____

Our next objective was:

■ to listen to employees during interviews.

Once the right sort of questions have been asked the first line manager must then listen to the answers. Listening is not an easy skill and is one that needs practice. Spend some time thinking about the following issues:

■ How will you show the employee that you are actively listening?

_____

_____

■ How competent are you at present at listening? How could you improve these skills?

_____

_____

The next objective that we covered in this workbook was:

■ to give effective feedback on performance.

People need to know how well they are doing and where they need to improve, therefore feedback is essential. The skill of giving feedback to workteam members is a skill all first line managers must develop. This feedback must be constructive and delivered in such a way that it is acceptable to the employee. At the end of the interview the employee must feel confident and motivated to improve. In considering this, please give some thought to:

■ the type of feedback you will give to your workteam members;

■ your own competence in delivering feedback.

The following objective was:

■ to draw up action plans.

It is essential that at the end of the appraisal interview the action that is agreed between line manager and employee be recorded in an action plan. This needs to record **what** will take place, **when**, **where** and **who** will be involved. This action plan must then be reviewed regularly. Before you finish this reflect and review section, please give some thought to the following issues.

■ What type of action plan should you draw up at the end of your interviews?

_____

_____

■ How will you review progress?

_____

_____

The next objective was:

■ to monitor performance against objectives.

Monitoring is an ongoing assessment activity which you should use to check that your team members are achieving the objectives agreed during the appraisal interview. When planning your monitoring approach you should keep in mind certain considerations.

■ How have team members been monitored in the past in your workplace?

_____

_____

■ Is there a better way of doing it which will increase the appraisees' motivation?

_____

_____

The penultimate objective was:

■ to select appropriate methods to improve performance where necessary.

One of the key purposes of appraisal is to identify ways in which a team member could improve performance. With this in mind consider the following.

■ How do team members currently acquire new skills identified as a result of an appraisal?

  _____

  _____

■ How can you find out what other training opportunities exist to enable appraisees to acquire new skills?

  _____

  _____

The final objective we examined was:

■ to complete appraisal documentation.

There are numerous ways in which appraisal information and findings can be recorded. We considered three main ways when we looked at comparison with objectives, ratings and narrative reporting. All the methods have advantages and disadvantages but perhaps the best system is one that combines all three and also includes an action plan. As part of your review process answer the following questions:

■ What appraisal documentation does your organization have at present?

  _____

  _____

■ What improvements could you make to existing documentation?

  _____

  _____

2 Action plan

Use this plan to further develop for yourself a course of action you want to take. Make a note in the left-hand column of the issues or problems you want to tackle, and then decide what you intend to do, and make a note in column 2.

The resources you need might include time, materials, information or money. You may need to negotiate for some of them, but they could be something easily acquired, like half an hour of somebody's time, or a chapter of a book. Put whatever you need in column 3. No plan means anything without a timescale, so put a realistic target completion date in column 4.

Finally, describe the outcome you want to achieve as a result of this plan, whether it is for your own benefit or advancement, or a more efficient way of doing things.

Desired outcomes				
	1 Issues	2 Action	3 Resources	4 Target completion
Actual outcomes				

3 Extensions

Extension 1

Book	*Effective Performance Appraisals*
Author	Robert B. Maddux
Publisher	Kogan Page, 1988

Extension 2

Video	*How Am I Doing?*
Publisher	Video Arts

Extension 3

Video	*The Dreaded Appraisal*
Publisher	Video Arts

Extension 4

Book	*Managing People* (Chapter 7)
Author	R. Cartwright, M. Collins, G. Green and A. Candy
Publisher	Blackwell, 1998

Extension 5

Video and workbook	*The Empowering Appraisal*
Publisher	BBC for Business

These extensions can be taken up via your ILM Centre. They will either have them or will arrange for you to have access to them. However, it may be more convenient to check out the materials with your personnel or training people at work – they may well give you access. There are other good reasons for approaching your own people; for example, they will become aware of your interest and you can involve them in your development.

If you already have someone supporting you through your development you may be able to discuss further reading materials with them.

4 Answers to self-assessment questions

Self-assessment 1 on pages 18–19

1 a Performance can be improved by appraisal, but that doesn't have to imply any **CRITICISM** of performance to date.

b The idea of performance appraisal can meet with a lot of **OPPOSITION**.

c Many **PEOPLE** who have to appraise staff oppose appraisals.

2 The main purposes or objectives of performance appraisal are:

a To evaluate staff training and development needs.

b To review past performance.

c To improve current and future performance.

d To assess potential.

e To help with career planning.

f To determine salary levels.

g To set performance objectives.

3 a We need to know certain things about the job before we can improve **PERFORMANCE** at work.

b Quantifying performance standards allows performance to be **MEASURED**.

c There can be problems in linking performance appraisal with **SALARY DECISIONS**.

d Making decisions about sharing out rewards in organizations can often lead to **CONFLICT** and **DIFFICULTIES**.

e A good salary review system should attempt to be **FAIR** and **JUST**.

4 An organization can ensure that its system of adjusting salaries is fair and just by:

- using an effective appraisal system;
- seeking staff views on the salary system;
- looking at salary structures and systems in other organizations;
- attempting to establish formulae and rules to determine salary increases.

Self assessment 2 on page 32

1 a To assess performance you need to decide HOW you are going to gather evidence

b Many appraisal interviews take place once a YEAR.

c Before an appraisal interview the appraiser should always BRIEF the appraisee.

d Before the interview you should gather information about the employee's PERSONAL QUALITIES and SKILLS.

2 Pre-appraisal is the process of briefing employees before the appraisal interview and providing them with a pre-appraisal form. The purpose is to enable them to prepare themselves for the appraisal interview.

3 Having a 'grandfather' as appraiser ensures fairness, provides an overview, maintains standards of assessment, gives a second opinion.

4 A performance standard is a statement that states the standard to which a performance objective must be carried out, for example by specifying 'how many', how often' or 'by when'. '

Self assessment 3 on page 59

1 An appraiser may need to gather the following information prior to running a performance appraisal interview:

- last year's appraisal documentation;
- the workteam member's job description;
- a list of objectives to be achieved during the interview;
- the views and opinions of any other interested parties;
- information about achievement against performance objectives, e.g. sales performance against targets, etc.

2 a Appraisers must ensure that they agree the **OBJECTIVES** of an appraisal interview with the individual concerned.
  b Appraisers must ensure that they collect **INFORMATION** about the appraisee's performance.
  c Appraisers should ensure there are no **INTERRUPTIONS**.

3 a If the appraiser is **WELL PREPARED** the appraisal interview will be more **EFFECTIVE**.
  b A first line manager carrying out an appraisal should encourage the individual to **TALK**.
  c Both during and after the appraisal interview the individual expects **FEEDBACK**.
  d Feedback should be **QUICK** and **REGULAR**.

4 An action plan should contain:

- recommended future action;
- the individual's training and development needs;
- resources required;
- the period of time concerned, e.g. six months;
- performance targets.

Self assessment 4 on page 69

1 The 'comparison with objectives' recording system compares current achievements with pre-set targets.

2 BARS stands for 'Behaviourally anchored rating scales'.

3 BOS stands for 'Behavioural observation scale'.

4 Employees may be suspicious, Appraisers can make judgements without having to justify them, the atmosphere of the department may be affected, it is more difficult for employees to improve their performance if the appraisal is kept secret.

5 Answers to activities

Activity 22 on page 40

We hope that you selected the **joint problem-solving** option for the main style of the interview. This option has the following benefits:

■ It uses the employee's own perceptions of his or her strengths and weaknesses and avoids any confrontation that may occur if the first line manager uses the **tell** option.
■ If the employee is involved in the solution generation process he or she will have far more commitment to and ownership of the solutions.
■ It allows the first line manager to listen to what the employee has to say before making any comments. This adds to the amount of evidence that is available to the first line manager.

6 Answers to the quick quiz

Answer 1   First line managers should be continuously assessing the performance of their workteams. Not just formally at the appraisal interview but all the time on a day-to-day basis.

Answer 2   An effective performance appraisal system is a candid communication process where both good and bad points are brought up and provision is made to maintain the good points and work on the bad points through training and development.

Answer 3   Although performance appraisal may indeed look back over a time period the main emphasis is on looking forward to motivate workteam members to maintain and improve performance.

Answer 4   It is absolutely essential for workteam members to know, in quantitative terms if possible, how well they are doing with their job and the standards that their first line managers expect of them.

Answer 5   It's vital that annual appraisals provide formal feedback but feedback is also a continuous ongoing process. It's no good, for example, a first line manager waiting until a formal appraisal to tell someone that they are displeased with something that happened eleven months ago.

Answer 6   Identifying the training needs of a workteam member is a very important part of an appraisal system because it helps to improve future performance.

Answer 7   Early appraisal systems focused on personality traits such as charisma and enthusiasm.

Answer 8   This type of system concentrates on personality characteristics and traits. The idea behind this is that people need to possess certain inherent characteristics to be good at certain jobs.

Answer 9   Employees are more likely to improve their future performance in an open system of appraisal because they will be more aware of what's expected of them and what the first line manager's opinion of their work is. They will also have played an active part in the appraisal.

Answer 10   Besides the first line manager, others who are likely to be interested in the results of an appraisal are the personnel department and senior managers.

Answer 11   No. If an appraisal system is to focus on job performance then the appraiser is likely to be much more effective if he or she knows about the job of the person being appraised.

Answer 12   The atmosphere in an appraisal interview is very important if the interview is to be constructive and forward looking, as it should be.

Answer 13   Preparation plays a very important part in an appraisal interview. In order to get the best results an appraiser has to take considerable care to plan the interview properly beforehand, for example by making sure that all the necessary facts are gathered, by making sure that the interview will not be interrupted and by giving other people the chance to make a well thought out contribution.

Answer 14   The purpose of feedback is to offer information about a person's BEHAVIOUR and PERFORMANCE. The process of NOTE-TAKING should not be allowed to DOMINATE the appraisal interview.

Answer 15   Three methods you could use to monitor team members' performance are: regular reviews, encouraging them to give informal feedback on their progress, observing by 'walking about'.

7 Certificate

Completion of this certificate by an authorized person shows that you have worked through all the parts of this workbook and satisfactorily completed the assessments. The certificate provides a record of what you have done that may be used for exemptions or as evidence of prior learning against other nationally certificated qualifications.

Pergamon Flexible Learning and ILM are always keen to refine and improve their products. One of the key sources of information to help this process are people who have just used the product. If you have any information or views, good or bad, please pass these on.

INSTITUTE OF LEADERSHIP & MANAGEMENT

SUPERSERIES

Appraising Performance

....

has satisfactorily completed this workbook

Name of signatory   ....

Position   ....

Signature   ....

Date   ....

Official stamp

Fourth Edition